All Families

Immigrant and Refugee Families

by Julie Kentner

www.focusreaders.com

Focus Readers is distributed by North Star Editions:
sales@northstareditions.com | 888-417-0195

Produced for Focus Readers by Red Line Editorial.

Photographs ©: iStockphoto, cover, 1, 4, 7, 8, 13, 14, 16, 19, 27, 29; Shutterstock Images, 11, 20–21, 22, 24

Library of Congress Cataloging-in-Publication Data
Library of Congress Cataloging-in-Publication Data is available on the Library of Congress website.

ISBN
978-1-63739-458-8 (hardcover)
978-1-63739-495-3 (paperback)
978-1-63739-567-7 (ebook pdf)
978-1-63739-532-5 (hosted ebook)

Printed in the United States of America
Mankato, MN
012023

About the Author

Julie Kentner is a writer who grew up in Boissevain, Manitoba. She loves history and research. She lives in Winnipeg with her husband and their cats.

Table of Contents

Chapter 1

A Big Move

The family was moving to a new country. The children had never been on a plane before. It was very exciting. When they landed, they talked to a woman at the airport. She asked them lots of questions.

More than 100,000 flights happen around the world every day.

Next, they got their luggage. Then the family went to their new house.

The children missed their cousins and grandparents in their old country. They also missed playing with their friends. They didn't know anyone at their new school. The other children even spoke a different language. It was hard to

Some people say dealing with a new country's weather can be hard.

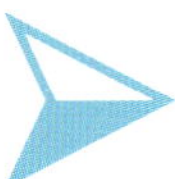

Students at new schools often struggle with feeling lonely.

understand. But every day, they learned a few more words.

It was both exciting and sad to move so far away. But the family was together.

Chapter 2

How It Works

Immigrant and refugee families both move to new countries. Both also plan to live in those countries. But immigrant and refugee families move for different reasons.

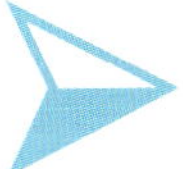

Many families cross the ocean to reach their new homes.

Immigrant families choose to move. They might move for better jobs or schools. In contrast, refugee families must move. They leave to stay safe. Some families become refugees because of war. Fighting might break out where they live. Extreme weather can be another

Extreme weather forces millions of people from their homes every year. And **climate change** is making extreme weather worse.

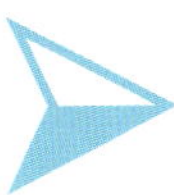

In late 2020, two hurricanes hit Central America. Many families had to leave their countries.

cause. Strong storms can destroy homes. Then families need to find new places to live.

Sometimes, families are able to move together. But others move at different times. For example, one parent might immigrate first.

In the new country, the parent works to earn money. The family saves up money. That money helps pay for the rest of the family to come.

Countries have systems for immigrants and refugees. They give permission for some people to stay. Each country has its own rules. For instance, some countries let people come for work or school.

Some people stay in a new country even if they do not have

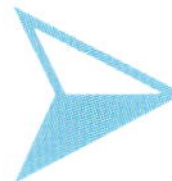

Refugee families often stay in camps while they wait for new homes. Many stay there for years.

permission. When that happens, they are **undocumented**. Some people come without stopping at the border. Others come with a **visa**. But they might stay longer than the visa allows.

Bienvenue
Welcome
Bienvenido
Benvenuto
欢迎
Willkommen
Bem-vindo
Добро
пожаловать
歡迎
Welkom
أهلاً وسهلاً
환영합니다

Chapter 3

Challenges

Immigrant and refugee families can face many challenges. For example, people might not have any family or friends in the new country. Families might have to learn a new language, too.

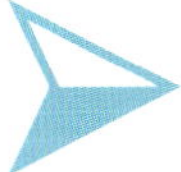

Thousands of different languages are spoken around the world.

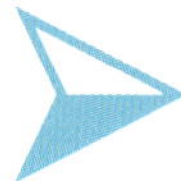

Some children help translate for their parents when they visit the doctor.

In fact, some children **translate** for their parents. They might help their parents use services. For instance, they might talk to people at the bank. This role places a lot of

responsibility on children. Children face other kinds of pressure, too. Parents might expect their children to be very successful. That can be because parents gave a lot up when they moved.

Many families also face **cultural** differences in new countries. People might practice different religions.

In the early 2020s, approximately 1 in 30 people were immigrants or refugees.

Popular music can be different, too. Children might find it hard to fit in. Plus, moving can also separate children from their own family's culture. So, children often struggle to feel like they're part of either one.

Mental health is another common struggle. Refugees might have seen scary events before leaving. And the journey to a new country can be dangerous. These experiences can cause **trauma**. This can last for a long time.

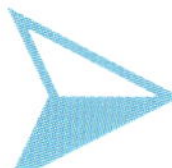
Kids often notice the worries of their parents.

Undocumented people face extra challenges. They might worry about being **deported**. This is stressful. It can also lead to avoiding services such as health care. That can mean health problems don't get treated.

Immigration and Race

Many countries have laws to make sure people are treated equally. But people often still face **racism** when they immigrate.

Racism causes many problems for families. It can make it harder for parents to find jobs. It can also make finding a home harder. Immigrant children often face racism, too. They might be bullied at school.

Racism is harmful over time as well. It can make it more difficult for people to trust others. It can also harm people's mental health.

Immigrant children are more likely to be bullied at school.

Chapter 4

Coming to a New Country

Immigrants and refugees leave many things behind when they move. They might leave their families and friends. Children might have to leave their favorite toys.

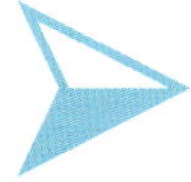

Many people can feel angry, guilty, or sad about leaving their home.

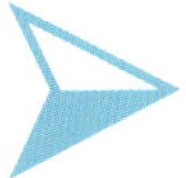

Some painful feelings lead to big behaviors. Others can make people feel frozen.

Children can have different feelings about immigration. Some might be excited for the new adventure. Other children may have seen war or death. They might be feeling sadness about a loss. All of these feelings are okay.

These feelings can come up at school. Immigrant and refugee children might struggle to pay attention. Or it might be hard to remember things. Students might also act in big ways during class.

People in the new country can help. They can treat immigrant and refugee families with compassion. They can show kindness. People can also be curious about new families' cultures. They can show they have a lot to learn, too.

That can help make families feel welcome. People can also help families get used to the new country. For instance, they can explain the country's culture.

Remembering where one comes from is also important. Immigrants and refugees can keep celebrating

In 2020, more than 50 million people in the United States were born somewhere else.

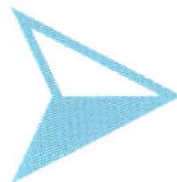

Many Mexican American families celebrate Día de Muertos, or Day of the Dead.

their own holidays. Or they can visit with other people from their old home. That way, they can hold on to their own culture.

FOCUS ON

Immigrant and Refugee Families

Write your answers on a separate piece of paper.

1. Write a paragraph explaining the main ideas of Chapter 2.
2. How would you describe the culture of your family?
3. What is one common cause of refugee families?
   - A. war
   - B. nice weather
   - C. good jobs
4. Why might a dangerous journey to a new country cause trauma?
   - A. Trauma only happens when traveling.
   - B. Traveling is always an easy experience.
   - C. Fear can last a long time after a dangerous event.

5. What does **compassion** mean in this book?

They can treat immigrant and refugee families with ***compassion****. They can show kindness.*

A. feeling alone or separated
B. feeling care and concern for others
C. feeling afraid of others

6. What does **pressure** mean in this book?

Children face other kinds of ***pressure****, too. Parents might expect their children to be very successful.*

A. feeling free
B. likely to fail
C. being pushed a certain way

Answer key on page 32.

Glossary

climate change
A human-caused global crisis involving long-term changes in Earth's temperature and weather patterns.

cultural
Having to do with a group of people and the way they live, including their customs, beliefs, and laws.

deported
Forced to leave a country.

racism
Hatred or mistreatment of people because of their skin color or ethnicity.

responsibility
Pressure to do or take care of something.

translate
To change words from one language to another.

trauma
A feeling of lasting fear and shock after a difficult experience.

undocumented
Not having the legal papers to show permission to be in a country.

visa
A type of legal permission to be in a country.

To Learn More

BOOKS

Burgan, Michael. *Immigrants Who Took a Stand*. North Mankato, MN: Capstone Press, 2021.

Lee, Jen Sookfong. *Finding Home: The Journey of Immigrants and Refugees*. Custer, WA: Orca Book Publishers, 2021.

Rosen, Michael. *Understanding Immigration*. New York: Rosen Publishing, 2020.

NOTE TO EDUCATORS

Visit **www.focusreaders.com** to find lesson plans, activities, links, and other resources related to this title.

Index

Answer Key: 1. Answers will vary; **2.** Answers will vary; **3.** A; **4.** C; **5.** B; **6.** C